MAY   1992   KN

track
athletics

robert sandelson

Crestwood House
New York

Maxwell Macmillan International
New York   Oxford   Singapore   Sydney

OLYMPIC SPORTS

OLYMPIC SPORTS

TRACK ATHLETICS
FIELD ATHLETICS
SWIMMING AND DIVING
GYMNASTICS
ICE SPORTS
SKIING
BALL SPORTS
COMBAT SPORTS

Designer: Ian Roberts
Editor: Deborah Elliott

Cover: 100-m final in Seoul, 1988.

CRESTWOOD HOUSE

Macmillan Publishing Company
866 Third Avenue
New York, NY 10022

Macmillan Publishing Company is part of the Maxwell Communication Group of Companies.

First published in Great Britain in 1991
by Wayland (Publishers) Ltd
61 Western Road, Hove, East Sussex BN3 1JD

Printed in Italy by G. Canale & C.S.p.A.
1 2 3 4 5 6 7 8 9 10

ACKNOWLEDGMENTS

The Publisher would like to thank the following agencies and photographers for allowing their pictures to be reproduced in this book: All-Sport UK Photographic Limited *cover*, 4 (Pascal Rondeau), 5 (bottom, Tony Duffy), 6, 9, 10 (Joe Patronite), 11 (top, Gray Mortimore) (bottom, Mike Powell), 13 (Gray Mortimore), 14, 15, 17 (Mike Powell), 18, 19 (both, Gray Mortimore), 20 (Billy Strickland), 21 (both, Tony Duffy), 22, 23 (Tony Duffy), 25, 26, 27, 29 (Tony Duffy), 31 (bottom, Tony Duffy), 32, 33, 34 (Tony Duffy), 36, 37 (Steve Powell), 38 (Tony Duffy), 41, 42, 43 (Bob Martin), 44 (Tony Duffy); Colorsport 8 (Philippe Caron), 16, 24, 28, 30, 31 (top), 35, 39, 42, 45; Mary Evans Picture Library 7.

Library of Congress Cataloging-in-Publication Data

Sandelson, Robert.
    Track athletics/Robert Sandelson.
        p.   cm. — (Olympic sports)
    Includes bibliographical references and index.
    Summary: An overview of the events that make up the track athletics portion of the Olympic Games, highlighting great athletes and moments related to the sports.
    ISBN 0-89686-671-8
    1. Track-athletics — Juvenile literature.
2. Running — Juvenile literature. 3. Olympics — Juvenile Literature. [1. Track and field. 2. Running. 3. Olympics.] I. Title. II. Series:
Olympic sports (Series)
GV1060.5.S24 1991
796.42—dc20 90-27449 CIP AC

CONTENTS

THE OLYMPIC IDEAL

"The most important thing in the Olympic Games is not to win but to take part, just as the most important thing in life is not the triumph but the struggle. The essential thing is not to have conquered but to have fought well."
—Baron Pierre de Coubertin

At any Olympic Games, the track events always take center stage. The sprints have captivated audiences since the first Games. They were held at Olympia in Greece 2,500 years ago. As soon as the starting gun fires, we watch to find out who the fastest men and women on earth are. At the other end of the scale are the long-distance events. These test a runner's strength and endurance. Finally there is the drama of the marathon. Even if we are only watching the events on television, there are few who do not share with the athletes the dream of winning an Olympic gold medal.

The founders of the modern Olympiad had a simple ideal. They believed that the Games should bring about friendly relations among the competing nations. But this has met with mixed success. Certainly among athletes individual friendships have

▼ The Olympic flame burning at the 1984 Los Angeles Games.

4

There was a mass boycott by the East European nations, with the exception of Romania. Fortunately the deadlock between East and West was broken for the 1988 Games in Seoul, Korea. Since then a new political situation has lessened the threat of another boycott.

◀ A huge audience witnessed the ceremony to open the Seoul Olympic Games in September 1988.

▼ Sebastian Coe is overcome with joy after winning the 1500 m in Moscow. Coe is now a prospective Member of Parliment (MP) for the British Conservative Party.

overcome political and national differences. Unfortunately, governments have not always done the same. For instance, after the Soviet invasion of Afghanistan in 1979, President Jimmy Carter asked athletes from the United States to boycott the 1980 Games to be held in Moscow. He even threatened to withdraw the passports of those athletes who tried to participate. Pressure was put on American allies, and the British government also requested its athletes not to go to Moscow. Some athletes ignored this call, most notably Sebastian Coe, Steve Ovett and Alan Wells, the 100-m gold medalist.

At the 1984 Games in Los Angeles, feelings of bitterness still existed.

THE 100 M

The Olympic male and female 100-m champions are widely recognized as the fastest men and women on earth. The world watches expectantly every four years to learn the identities of the people who will win these titles.

The 100-m race is the most delicate and finely tuned event of all. Some athletes hope to become Olympic champions in this field. They must have strength, lightning reflexes, perfect balance and determination.

Harold Abrahams was Great Britain's first great Olympic sprinter. He led a new age in the 100 m when he went into intensive training for the Paris Games of 1924. Abrahams' perform-ance set a new standard in physical fitness. His victory meant that after-wards only maximum determination would see an athlete through to victory. The story of his training was dramatized in the movie *Chariots of Fire*.

▼ Harold Abrahams (second from right) won the 100 m for Great Britain at the 1924 Paris Games.

The hallmark of the greatest sprinters from Abrahams on is their incredible dedication. Archie Hahn, "The Milwaukee Meteor," Charley Paddock, "The World's Fastest Human," Eddie Tolan, "The Midnight Express," and many others have stunned the world by incredible displays of human speed.

The 100 m is one of two women's track events that have an Olympic history dating back to before World War I. That history is full of amazing achievements and bitter controversies. In the 1930s there was a great rivalry between Stanislawa Walasiewicz, a resident of the United States who ran for Poland under the name of Stella Walsh, and American Helen Stephens.

Walsh had won the 100 m in Los Angeles in 1932. She found her supremacy challenged in the following years by the young contender. When the pair reached Berlin in 1936, Stephens was the firm favorite because she held the new world record. Much to Walsh's disappointment, Stephens performed well and took the gold medal. In doing so she earned the dubious pleasure of an audience with Adolf Hitler. He asked her to spend the weekend with him — an offer she turned down!

Walsh never had another chance to reclaim her title since Stephens soon retired, undefeated in running events. Such was the bad feeling between the two athletes and their supporters that a Polish journalist accused Stephens of being a man. Oddly enough this accusation backfired. When Stella Walsh died, 44 years later, it was discovered that she was, after all, a man!

One of the greatest female athletes of all times was Fanny Blankers-Koen from the Netherlands. As an 18-year-old she was selected to compete at the 1936 Berlin Games, but she won no medals. Because of World War II she had to wait another 12 years for her next chance at Olympic glory. By then, however, she was considered over the hill at the age of 30.

▲ Fanny Blankers-Koen — the Netherlands' greatest-ever female athlete.

Blankers-Koen did not by any means have an easy road to the 1948 London Games. She felt pressured by the high expectations of her nation. In the years before the Games she had been incredibly dedicated. This dedication was reinforced when, three weeks after the birth of her second child in 1946, she came out of retirement. She took the baby to meets all over Europe, on an Olympic trail that ended in London two years later. Blankers-Koen proved her critics wrong by winning four events. These included the 100 m in the fast time of 11.9 seconds (on a slow track) and by the clear margin of 2.7 m (0.3 second).

The first athlete to win the gold medal in the 100 m in consecutive Olympic Games was Wyomia Tyus of the United States. She won at Tokyo in 1964 and again at Mexico City in 1968. It was another 20 years before this feat was equaled by Carl Lewis. To win once is hard but twice is so much harder. It must have seemed impossible to Tyus as she stood in the blocks for a final that featured four world record holders. The rain was beating down in Mexico City, the gun was raised and Tyus was off. Unfortunately, the athletes were called back to the starting blocks because of a false start. Down they went again and this time they started well. The champion with the confidence and speed to beat the world did just that.

▶ The 100-m sprinters in full flow.

▼ Ben Johnson (center) flies off the blocks at the start of the 100 m.

Lewis versus Johnson

The eight runners who had qualified for the final of the 100 m made their way to the track on Saturday, September 24, 1988, in Seoul. They were making their way into the history books as the participants in one of the greatest races ever run.

The event had reached a fever pitch as the competition between two great rivals reached a climax. Carl Lewis of the United States had been four times gold medalist at the Los Angeles Games in 1984. He walked out to face Ben Johnson of Canada, world champion and world record holder.

Since the 1984 Games, Ben Johnson had been steadily improving. In the World Championships in Rome in 1987, he had beaten the opposition and the world record with a run of 9.83 seconds. Carl Lewis, on the other hand, had everything to run for because no

man had ever had a better chance to win the coveted gold medal twice. Also participating were former world record holder American Calvin Smith and Great Britain's hope, Linford Christie, a veteran at 28. Both of them had easily qualified for the final.

Ten seconds is not a long time, but moments after the starting gun was fired, the spectators knew that this was going to be the most extraordinary 10 seconds in Olympic history. Ben Johnson, without a hint of a false start, had flown off the blocks. He made the others look as though they were contestants in a three-legged race. Calvin Smith, Carl Lewis and Linford Christie, though pulling clear of the rest of the field, were all looking at one man's back. At about 70 m Johnson turned his head, saw Lewis behind him and raised his arm to acknowledge the amazed shouts of the crowd. At the

▲ Carl Lewis (center) looks on in surprise as Ben Johnson storms away from the rest of the field.

end he even seemed to slow down! Behind him Carl Lewis was fighting off a challenge from Christie. Christie himself was ensuring third place by finishing before Smith. Then all eyes turned to the clock — 9.79 seconds. This was a staggering performance considering the 9.83 seconds of the previous year. That time was so amazing that one expert predicted that the record would stand for at least 50 years!

When the race was over, everyone assumed that this concluded one of the greatest rivalries in modern Olympic history and that Lewis had been beaten by the faster sprinter. But 24 hours later, the world was shocked when the truth about Ben Johnson's performance was revealed .

Johnson was tested for drugs. The test was positive and he was stripped of his title. His career was ruined. His world records were invalidated. Carl Lewis was named the Olympic champion and became the holder of a world record for the first time. Linford Christie had been the first European to break the 10-second

Evelyn Ashford and Florence Griffith Joyner (Flo-Jo) have dominated the women's 100 m. Their times at the Olympic Games have been better than many of the men's. Indeed Flo-Jo's winning time in Seoul was faster than those of the runners in the men's quarter-finals.

◀ Carl Lewis, Ben Johnson and Linford Christie at the 100-m medal ceremony. Johnson was later disqualified for taking drugs.

▼ Florence Griffith Joyner of the United States acknowledges the crowd after winning the women's 100 m.

barrier with 9.97 seconds. He was awarded the silver, and Smith took the bronze medal.

By cheating, Ben Johnson ruined dedication to training that had started with Abrahams. The desire to win rose above all other considerations, even the spirit of the Olympics. The greatest race in Olympic history had ended in shame for one man and the nation he represented. But there was triumph for Carl Lewis, the first man ever to retain his title, and the other two runners. They all recorded sub-10-second times to make it the fastest race in Olympic, indeed all, history.

In recent years, runners like Merlene Ottey of Jamaica and Americans

Olympic Champions		Country	Seconds
1896	Thomas Burke	USA	12
1900	Frank Jarvis	USA	11
1904	Archie Hahn	USA	11
1908	Reginald Walker	South Africa	10.8
1912	Ralph Craig	USA	10.8
1920	Charles Paddock	USA	10.8
1924	Harold Abrahams	Great Britain	10.6
1928	Percy Williams	Canada	10.8
1932	Eddie Tolan	USA	10.3
1936	Jesse Owens	USA	10.3
1948	Harrison Dillard	USA	10.3
1952	Lindy Remigino	USA	10.4
1956	Bobby Joe Morrow	USA	10.5
1960	Armin Hary	Germany	10.2
1964	Robert Hayes	USA	10.06
1968	Jim Hines	USA	9.95
1972	Valery Borzov	USSR	10.14
1976	Hasely Crawford	Trinidad	10.06
1980	Allan Wells	Great Britain	10.25
1984	Carl Lewis	USA	9.99
1988	Carl Lewis	USA	9.92
1928	Elizabeth Robinson	USA	12.2
1932	Stella Walsh	Poland	11.9
1936	Helen Stephens	USA	11.5
1938	Fanny Blankers-Koen	Netherlands	11.9
1952	Marjorie Jackson	Australia	11.5
1956	Betty Cuthbert	Australia	11.5
1960	Wilma Rudolph	USA	11.0
1964	Wyomia Tyus	USA	11.4
1968	Wyomia Tyus	USA	11.0
1972	Renate Stecher	East Germany	11.07
1976	Annagret Richter	East Germany	11.08
1980	Lyudmila Kondratyeva	USSR	11.06
1984	Evelyn Ashford	USA	10.97
1988	Florence Griffith Joyner	USA	10.54

THE 200 M

In some ways the 200 m is even more exciting than the 100 m. When the athletes come off the bend, the display of speed and power is awe-inspiring.

From 1932 until 1948, women athletes were not allowed to compete over distances longer than 100 m at the Olympic Games. In 1935 Stella Walsh set one of the fastest track records in the 200 m. It lasted for 17 years. When the event was first staged at the London Olympics in 1948, Fanny Blankers-Koen of the Netherlands won the title.

In the past, 100-m runners have often performed well in the 200 m. However, today it is by no means guaranteed. More and more, the two events are becoming specialized. Joe Deloach of the United States showed this trend by his victory in Seoul in 1988. He beat his training partner, Carl Lewis, in the Olympic record time of 19.75 seconds. His performance showed that special concentration on one sprint event might well mean that "the double" is a thing of the past.

One athlete who did win the double with particular ease was the great black American Jesse Owens. Owens, whose grandparents had been slaves in the South, was a phenomenon in the world of athletics. On May 25, 1935, at the age of only 21, Owens set five track and field world records between 3:15 P.M. and 4 P.M. At the Olympic Games in Berlin the following year, he won the 200-m final by a clear 3 m in an Olympic record time of 20.7 seconds.

The Berlin Games, however, will not only be remembered for Owens's brilliance. The Games were the most notorious example of the manipulation of the Olympics for the purposes of

▲ The eventual winner of the 200 m, Joe Deloach of the United States, storms around the bend in the final in Seoul in 1988.

propaganda. Adolf Hitler, Germany's fascist leader, held the racist view that black people were inferior to white, or Aryan, races. Hitler hoped that the Olympic Games could be used to demonstrate this view. The arena was filled with swastikas and the fascist flag. And the hostility toward black athletes was evident everywhere. When the racing started, it became obvious that the 10 black American track athletes, and Jesse Owens in particular, were going to destroy

▲ Jesse Owens at the 1936 Olympic Games in Berlin.

▶ Valery Borzov of the Soviet Union in Munich, 1972.

Hitler's plans. They won no less than seven gold, three silver and three bronze medals among them. Owens's ability was so awesome that his triumphs were applauded by the Germans themselves, and Hitler's anger was evident.

American male athletes have had an amazing record in the short track distances. Six of them have won the 100-m and 200-m double. The achievement of a non-American, Valery Borzov of the Soviet Union, is particularly impressive. At Munich in 1972 he had an easy run in the 100 m. His closest rivals failed to qualify because they were late for the race — not the finishing line. American athletes Eddie Hart and Ray Robinson both timed at 9.9 seconds in the American Olympic trials. They missed their race because their coach was using an out-of-date train schedule. Although they were rushed to the stadium, they did not make it on time. Any thoughts that Borzov was an unworthy winner were blown away by his performance in the 200 m. He won the race in a European record time of 20.0 seconds.

At center stage in Seoul in 1988 was the thrilling Florence Griffith Joyner. She stunned the world by lowering the women's 200-m world record twice, in the semifinal and final. After nine years Marita Koch's world record of 21.71 seconds was smashed twice in the course of one day by Flo-Jo. Koch's record had been equaled once — by Heike Dreschler of East Germany. In the semifinal Flo-Jo ran a staggering 21.56 seconds. Within two hours she had even overshadowed this performance with the truly amazing time of 21.34 seconds. She reduced the record finally by 0.37 second. This was the first time that any sprinter had broken the world record twice in one day.

Flo-Jo and her sister-in-law, Jackie Joyner-Kersee, made the women's events a family affair. Joyner-Kersee set the world record in the heptathlon, a series of seven track and field events. She also won the long jump. Flo-Jo picked up golds for the 100 m and the 4×100 m relay and a silver in the 4×400 m relay.

▲ The brilliant Jamaican sprinter Grace Jackson competing in the 200 m in Seoul. Jamaica has consistently produced world-class sprinters.

► Flo-Jo salutes in triumph after winning the 200 m in Seoul.

THE 400 M

There is no race quite like the 400 m. Most athletes talk about it with strong feeling. The current world record holder, American Butch Reynolds, said: "The 400 m is a hard race, which you don't run too often because it ages you so quickly." Although no one was thought able to sprint this far, athletes are now expected to run as fast as 200-m runners to win. Competitors try to run a tactical race with a close eye on the clock. But ultimately tactics are forgotten in the Olympic final as extra reserves of strength, stamina and physical courage separate the medalists from the rest of the field.

The most remarkable gold medalist of his time was Eric Liddell of Great Britain. He learned only months before the 1924 Paris Olympics that the 100-m final was scheduled for a Sunday. Liddell, a devout Christian, decided to change events and move up to the 400 m. The Scotsman's faith paid off when he ran the race of his life to win the gold. Fifty-six years later another Scot, Allan Wells, won the 100 m at the 1980 Moscow Games. He cited the bravery and brilliance of this original "Flying Scot" as the inspiration behind his success.

Another great 400 m was run in Mexico City in 1968 by Lee Evans of the United States. Evans broke his own world record of 44.0 seconds with an amazing 43.86 seconds. His time also stood as a world record until Butch Reynolds smashed it in the season before Seoul. Reynolds ran 43.29 seconds in Zurich to make himself the Olympic favorite.

▶ Eric Liddell crosses the line in first place in the 400-m final at the Paris Games in 1924.

Reynolds had strong competition at Seoul from countrymen Steve Lewis, who was only 19 years old, and Danny Everett. The heats were all very fast. But when the final came there were no surprises in the lineup. Reynolds went off slowly compared with Lewis and Everett, preferring a more even-paced run. But at 300 m it was clear that an upset was in the cards. Reynolds found himself lagging in fourth place, almost 0.5 second behind the leader. It was too much to make up. Although he had the strength, the track was running out. He caught only three out of the four men ahead, finishing second in 43.93 seconds.

Steve Lewis, the youngest Olympic champion in 16 years, had finished in 43.87 seconds, which was 0.01 second behind Lee Evans's record. Butch Reynolds had run the fastest losing time in history. But this was hardly consolation for losing the race and the gold medal.

▲ Butch Reynolds of the United States was the favorite to win the gold medal in Seoul. However, he misjudged the pace of the race and finished in second place.

◀ Steve Lewis was the surprise winner of the 400 m in Seoul.

The women's 400-m event has been staged only seven times in Olympic history, beginning in Tokyo in 1964. The event has seen some great performers. Irena Szewinska was an outstanding athlete who won medals in four consecutive Olympic Games in the 100 m, 200 m, long jump and 100-m relay. In 1974 she became the first woman to break the 50-second barrier for the 400 m. This record was then broken by Christine Brehmer of East Germany, who was 12 years her junior. Szewinska finally met Brehmer for an eagerly awaited showdown in Montreal in 1976. In the race of her life, Szewinska flew around the last bend to beat Brehmer. She won by more than 10 m and set another world record time of 49.29 seconds.

▲ Debbie Flintoff-King of Australia (second from the left) winning the 400 m in Seoul.

Marita Koch of East Germany also stands out as a great athlete in this event. One of the most consistent athletes ever, Koch was a top-class sprinter for no less than 12 years. A lightning-fast runner, she broke the world record at the 400 m seven times. But the greatest athletes are always the ones who are able to overcome the trials of injury and stress. Koch was to face the disappointment of having to withdraw from the semifinal of the Montreal Olympics due to injury. Along with Brehmer and Szewinska she had had medal hopes. Fortunately she had the strength and determination to rebound from this setback. She was

▲ Irena Szewinska (left) and Marita Koch battle for first place in Moscow in 1980.

► East German Marita Koch won the gold in Moscow in 1980.

rewarded in Moscow in 1980 when she was able to triumph at least once in the place where it matters most to athletes. Another gold could well have been hers, but she was unable to attend the Games in Los Angeles in 1984, when she was the world record holder at 47.60 seconds. Her victory in Moscow, though, will never be forgotten. It was run at such a pace that the first three athletes finished in under 50 seconds—a unique performance in Olympic history.

THE 800 M

This distance was standardized in Antwerp in 1920. Until then it had been 880 yards (approx 803 m) or half a mile (approx 805 m). In Stockholm in 1912, Ted Meredith ran a record time for the 800 m. He then continued until the 880-yard mark, which he also crossed in record-breaking time.

The women's 800 m was first run at Olympic level in Amsterdam in 1928. It changed the face of women's athletics for 50 years. Lina Radke of Germany won in a world record time of 2:16.8 minutes.

It was such a fast race — the top three broke the world record — that many competitors collapsed from

▼ Ted Meredith winning the 800 m in Stockholm in 1912.

exhaustion. The press made a fuss about this, and ''experts'' were called in to back arguments that women should not compete over such long distances.

The prejudice underlying these arguments was obvious. Men had also suffered from exhaustion over this distance. But the male supporters were effective and the consequences were devastating.

Following this 1928 race no women's event longer than 200 m was run for 32 years at the Olympics. Three generations of women middle-distance runners have been lost from Olympic history. For great women athletes, like Nina Otkalenko of the Soviet Union, this ban must surely have cost them

▲ Anne Packer of Great Britain won a surprise victory in the 800 m at the Tokyo Games in 1964. This reduced the world record to 2:01.1 minutes.

Olympic gold medals. Between 1951 and 1955, Otkalenko took the world 800-m record down from 2:12.0 to 2:05.0 minutes. For countless other women athletes, this ban has been a pointless and humiliating episode in Olympic history.

The 800 m was reintroduced in Rome in 1960. One of the great surprise victors of this race was Ann Packer of Great Britain in Tokyo, 1964. She had finished fifth in her opening heat and third in her semifinal. Apparently, disappointed with her performance, she considered skipping the final in favor of doing some shopping! Luckily she changed her mind and, to her own and the whole world's surprise, won the gold.

Alberto Juantorena of Cuba left his indelible mark on this event when, as the world's top runner at the 400 m in 1976, he turned his attention to the 800 m. The two events had never been conquered by one runner. The physical strains are commonly considered to be too great.

The first man to approach the double had been Mal Whitfield of the United States. Between June 1948 and September 1954, he lost only 3 out of 69 races. He enjoyed long years of competition with Jamaican Arthur Wint at both distances. At the Olympics in 1948, Wint beat him into third place in the 400 m after Whitfield beat him at 800 m. Whitfield repeated this success in 1952.

But it took a very special athlete, Juantorena, to link these two titles. His belief that he would win the 400 m led him to take up the challenge of the 800 m. Unexpectedly, his long-stepping sprinter's style did not falter as he powered his way to the front after 300 m. To the amazement of the specialists, he remained there. Young Steve Ovett's fifth-place time was itself world class.

In the 1970s, two exceptional runners started one of the most remarkable rivalries at middle-distance running. Sebastian Coe and Steve Ovett, both of Great Britain, were breaking each other's world records with stunning regularity at the 1500-m,

▲ "White Lightning" — this was the name given to the superb Cuban 400-m and 800-m runner, Alberto Juantorena, after winning both events in Montreal in 1976.

1000-m, mile and 800-m distances.

The 800-m final in the 1980 Moscow Games looked like the rivalry might be over after all. Ovett and Coe had not faced each other for two years. The race, in the tradition of great finals, was not particularly fast. But it was hard fought and tense. Ovett and Coe ran slowly through the first lap and placed at sixth and eighth (last). Ovett quickly began to show his form. With elbows flying, he battled into second place. A confused Coe made his move too late and could not catch Ovett in the homestretch. Ovett's winning time was identical to his Montreal time. Coe's defeat left him devastated. But he would have a chance to answer his critics in the 1500 m six days later in a race that Ovett declared himself 90 percent sure of winning.

▲ Steve Ovett makes the decisive break in the final of the 800 m in the Moscow Games in 1980.

► Steve Ovett salutes his victory in Moscow in 1980.

THE 1500 M

The metric mile, as the 1500 m is also known, is a fascinating contest of stamina, tactics, positioning and race sense. The event is one of the most eagerly awaited in the competition. Olympic 1500-m finals are famous more for the quality of the racing than the final times. Because each runner is trying to gain positional and mental advantage, these are often outside the world record.

One of the best-known 1500-m races took place in Mexico City in 1968. Kip Keino, the Kenyan athlete, knew that his opponent, American James Ryun, had a better finishing sprint, so Keino went out much faster from the start. When Ryun "kicked," he was unable to make up the gap. Demoralized and overstretched, he dropped back. Keino won by the record margin of 20 m. On the day of the 1500-m final, Keino was caught in a traffic jam and had to jog 1.5 km to the stadium. This warm-up run proved helpful—he won the race!

To end a career unbeaten is rare, and an Australian, Herb Elliot, is the best-known runner to have earned such a distinction. Elliott retired early, at the age of only 22 (some say before his peak). Until then he ran at the highest level, never refusing a challenge. In the 1960 Rome Games he ran one of the most determined 1500-m races ever seen. His goal was a gold medal *and* a world record time. After 800 m, he realized that, if he was to stay at record pace, he would have to run alone. From here on, as he left the other runners behind, he never looked back once. He concentrated only on the finish line. He won in a world record time of 3:35.6 minutes. One of the other runners said Elliot took off like a "scared bunny."

▲ The brilliant Kenyan middle-distance runner, Kip Keino.

▲ Australian Herb Elliott was considered unbeatable in the mile.

One of the most talked about finals in Olympic history happened in the 1980 Moscow Games. Steve Ovett and Sebastian Coe met for the second time in six days. After his defeat in the 800 m, Coe was under enormous pressure to redeem himself. He needed to run the race of a lifetime to win the gold. However, Ovett, winner over this distance on 42 consecutive occasions, was the firm favorite.

The first three laps were closely fought with Ovett, Coe and Jurgen Straub of East Germany leading. Coe ran from the front to avoid being boxed in, as he had been in the 800 m. He sprinted for the tape with 200 m to go. Ovett followed him but lacked both the power in his legs and Coe's will to win. With a gold medal each, the two rivals had been united by Olympic glory. Four years later in Los Angeles, Coe became the first man in Olympic history to defend the 1500-m title.

▲ ▼ Above and below: Sebastian Coe in the 1500 m in Moscow.

▲ In the early 1970s the women's 1500 m was dominated by the Soviet athlete Lyudmila Bragina (left).

Women did not compete in an Olympic 1500-m race until Munich in 1972. At first it was dominated by Lyudmila Bragina of the Soviet Union. She was unknown in the West until six weeks before the Games. Then she reduced the world record by 2.7 seconds and became a favorite for the gold medal. In the final she ran away with the race after leaving her competitors in her wake with one lap to go.

The 1500 m requires as much planning as it does pure speed. Bragina found this out four years later during the 1976 Montreal Games. She was boxed in and unable to unleash her speed, and could do no better than fifth place in a slow race. This was the same race that saw the victory of Tatyana Kazankina of the Soviet Union. She went on to win a second gold medal at that distance in Moscow in 1980.

THE 3000 M

Slowly the Olympic authorities were forced to listen to the loud protests of women runners from all over the world. They were, rightly, angry at the absurd lack of distance track events open to them. Unbelievably, in 1980, the longest event open to women was the 1500 m. Eventually it was agreed to add a 3000-m event.

The Los Angeles 1984 Games were the first to host the 3000 m. The race was won by a Romanian, Maricica Puica. Those are the simple facts, but they don't even hint at the dramas of the race. This "first" saw one of the most infamous collisions in Olympic history.

This event drew the greatest middle-distance runners of the day like a magnet. Everyone wanted a chance at an Olympic medal. The lineup for the final included the popular American champion, Mary Decker-Slaney, Maricica Puica, and cross-country champion and the new 5000-m world record holder, Zola Budd. Budd's appearance was eagerly awaited. She was extraordinary for many reasons apart from her speed and habit of running barefoot. Although she was born in South Africa she had recently qualified to run for Great Britain. This decision caused some controversy.

Budd's speed at the age of 17 had brought her to world prominence in the 1984 Olympic year. Mary Decker-Slaney, on the other hand, was Budd's childhood hero, having won everything except an Olympic title. Now, surely she would fill this gap on her trophy shelf.

It was not to be. Both Decker-Slaney and Budd vied for the lead. In a tragic accident halfway through the race, Decker-Slaney tangled with Budd's

▲ Maricica Puica (right) of Romania won the 3000-m gold medal in Los Angeles in 1984.

Soviet Union. Third-place Yvonne Murray became the first Scotswoman to win an individual Olympic medal.

◀ Mary Decker-Slaney and Zola Budd were involved in one of the most controversial incidents in Olympic history, when Budd accidentally caused Decker-Slaney to trip during the 3000-m final.

▼ A distraught Mary Decker-Slaney is led away in tears after her Olympic dream was brought to an unfortunate end in 1984.

legs and fell. Injured, she was carried off in tears. Budd was badly distracted but managed to hold on to the lead. Then, with 300 m to go, Wendy Sly of Great Britain and Puica kicked past the rapidly fading Budd. Puica pulled clear of her rival 100 m later. Puica won the gold and Wendy Sly the silver medal in a race that is remembered more for its disappoint-ments than its result.

Four years later, in Seoul, the race was won by Tatyana Samolenko of the

THE 5000 M AND 10,000 M

T here are many great names associated with these events. The best runners have traditionally excelled at both distances. Men such as Emile Zatopek of Czechoslovakia and Paavo Nurmi and Lasse Viren of Finland were famous for their amazing stamina developed by grueling training.

Paavo Nurmi was a phenomenon. Between 1920 and 1928, he won nine gold and three silver medals.

Emile Zatopek easily won the 10,000 m in 1948 in London. In doing so he seemed the favorite for the 5000-m gold medal. The next day, along with his rival Gaston Reiff of Belgium, he qualified for the 5000-m final. On this occasion Reiff, three laps from the finish, surged ahead. Going into the last lap he had a 36.5-m lead over Zatopek, who appeared to be tired from the 10,000 m. However, as they entered the last 200 m, the Czech suddenly started to sprint. Reiff, with no extra reserves, could only struggle on as the shouts of the crowd told him of the late surge by his rival. The gap narrowed quickly, but Zatopek had made his dash too late and Reiff held on. Four years later in Helsinki, Zatopek avenged himself and won both titles.

The 5000 m in Helsinki, however, was not without its share of drama. About 300 m from the tape, Zatopek sprinted but was immediately caught and passed by three others. The last 200 m saw him fight back to win the most difficult victory of his career. Tiredness did not seem to affect Zatopek—he won the marathon, too!

▲ The superb Czechoslovakian distance runner Emile Zatopek in 1952 in Helsinki.

▶ Paavo Nurmi of Finland winning one of five Olympic gold medals in 1928. These included the 10,000 m and 5000 m.

Lasse Viren, a Finnish police officer, completed the ''double double'' in Montreal in 1976. He won the titles at 5000 m and 10,000 m, as he had done in Munich four years earlier. In the 10,000 m in 1972, Viren showed his unique quality of determination. After falling, he got himself back in the race and went through to win in a world record time. This unique feat has ensured him a place as one of the truly great Olympians, placing him alongside the other great Finnish runner, Paavo Nurmi.

After the inclusion of the women's marathon in 1984, the continued lack of a women's 10,000 m appeared ridiculous. After all, it was only a quarter of the distance of a marathon. It was announced that the first race at 10,000 m would be held in Seoul in 1988. This meant Olympic opportunities for record breakers such as Ingrid Kristiansen of Norway and Liz McColgan of Great Britain—the only woman to have beaten Kristiansen over 10,000 m. Liz McColgan, as the one genuine gold medal hope in the Great Britain team, had enormous pressure on her. The pressure was even greater because of the threat posed by Olga Bondarenko of the Soviet Union.

Once more, the unique strain of Olympic competition caused a big upset. Kristiansen, injured in a fast heat, had to drop out of the competition. In the final, McColgan was mercilessly shadowed by Bondarenko. Whether she ran faster or slower, she was unable to shake off the challenge of her rival. With only 200 m remaining in the race, the Russian kicked past her to victory.

▼ Lasse Viren (number 301) crosses the line to victory in the 5000-m final.

▲ Liz McColgan (right) of Great Britain and
Olga Bondarenko of the Soviet Union grimace as
they battle it out in the 10,000-m final in Seoul.

THE MARATHON

The marathon is a road race fixed at 42,195 m, or 26 miles 385 yards. The event was created for the modern Olympic movement in 1896 and has been a cornerstone ever since.

The early days of the Olympic marathon caused some of the greatest triumphs and controversies in Olympic history. The first marathon, in Athens, 1896, was appropriately won by a Greek, Spiridon Loves.

▼ Dorando Pietri is carried off on a stretcher after the marathon.

The London Games of 1908 saw the most remarkable of all finishes. Dorando Pietri of Italy collapsed on entry to the stadium. Eventually he was carried over the finishing line. The second athlete to finish, American John Hayes, rightly protested and was awarded the gold medal. However, Pietri went on to become an inter-

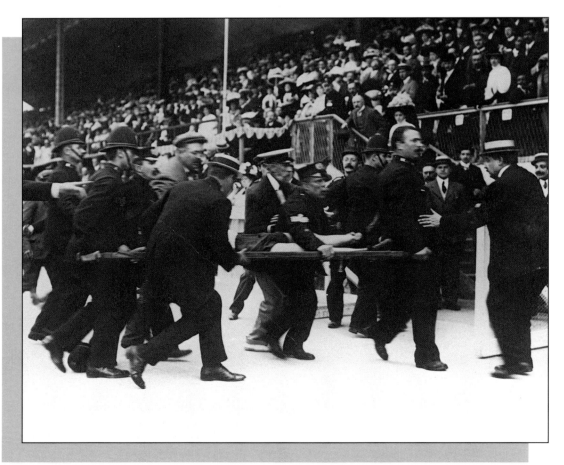

national celebrity. This made up somewhat for coming so close to the Olympic gold.

In Helsinki in 1952, Emile Zatopek, the Czech hero of the 5000-m and 10,000-m distances, decided to compete in the marathon. He hoped to achieve a unique triple. This decision amazed a world that was used to Zatopek's achievements. He had never run the distance in competition before. At the start of the race, he looked for the top marathon runner of the day, Jim Peters of Great Britain. After shadowing him for the first 16 km, Zatopek decided that he had the hang of it and skipped off to win the gold easily.

There has always been a struggle for women to be allowed to compete in runs of this distance. The long history of men collapsing in or after the marathon was conveniently forgotten when the women's race was discussed. Since the 1970s, however, women have taken great strides in the marathon event.

In 1972, the organizers allowed women to take part in the Boston marathon for the first time. Their finishing times began to improve rapidly. The popularity of the event was soon booming. It was in this context that the IOC (International Olympic Committee) included the event in the timetable for the Los Angeles Games in 1984.

► Grete Waitz of Norway was one of the top contenders for a medal in Seoul.

The great women marathon runners were all there: Rosa Mota, the European champion from Portugal; Grete Waitz of Norway, who had become world famous for her fast runs in the New York marathon; fellow Norwegian Ingrid Kristiansen; and the marathon world record holder, local heroine Joan Benoit. To marathon runners, times and world records are less important than results. They race against each other rather than the clock. The athletes must have a keen sense of all of their competitors' abilities as well as their own.

The Los Angeles marathon was much awaited. The race did not disappoint the crowd as Joan Benoit pulled away from the rest of the field. She was able to hold off a challenge from Waitz, who made her final kick too late. In turn, Waitz had left Mota and Kristiansen to fight for the bronze medal. Mota won the duel and four years later won in Seoul.

The race in Seoul boasted some of the world's fastest marathon runners. Mota, Waitz, Kathrin Doerre of East Germany and Lisa Martin of Australia had all run under 2.26.00 hours.

There is no doubt that prejudice against women runners still exists. This was nowhere more apparent than in the reaction to Gabriela Andersen-Schiess of Switzerland. In Seoul, suffering from the exceptional heat, she finished with obvious physical difficulty. The medalists, however, quickly dismissed any suggestion of female frailty. Such prejudice has now been confronted with new scientific evidence that women's bodies are better able than men's to cope with the extreme strains of long-distance running.

▶ The top contenders for the gold medal in Seoul in 1988 were Greta Waitz (Norway) and Rosa Mota (Portugal), together with Lisa Martin (Australia) and Kathrin Doerre (East Germany) — all proven sub-2.26.00-hour marathon runners. Mota gradually drew away from the other runners after the halfway mark and romped home to victory in 2.25.40 hours.

▲ The Los Angeles 1984 marathon was won by local athlete Joan Benoit. She set off at an extremely fast pace and then hung on to win in 2.24.52 hours.

HURDLES

The three major hurdle competitions at the Olympic Games are the 100-m hurdles for women and the 110-m and 400-m hurdles for men.

The 110-m Hurdles

Two men have won this race on two occasions: American Lee Calhoun in Melbourne in 1956 and Rome in 1964 and American Roger Kingdom in Los Angeles in 1984 and Seoul in 1988.

Before the Seoul Olympics the competition was intense between Olympic gold medalist Kingdom and Great Britain's Colin Jackson. In the final, Kingdom won and Jackson became Wales' first track medal winner since 1952, winning the silver.

The 100-m Hurdles
(before 1972, 80 m)

The 1930s and 1940s saw the heyday of the all-rounders. These were athletes who were able to run, jump and throw equally at the highest level. In women's events this was especially true. Along with Fanny Blankers-Koen from the Netherlands, the American Mildred ''Babe'' Didrikson dominated several events.

Babe came from a poor, immigrant Norwegian family from Texas. At the age of 16 she was spotted by a scout. He immediately recognized her strength and swiftness. She made history when, in the Olympic trials for the Los Angeles Games of 1932, she won the long jump, hurdles, shot put and javelin (with a new world record). She also tied in the high jump at a new world record — all in a single afternoon!

At the Olympics, much to her annoyance, Babe was restricted to participating in only three events. However, she showed her talent immediately by winning the javelin. Her second of three chosen events was the 80-m hurdles. She was competing against another great American hurdler,

◀ Winner of the 110-m-hurdles gold medal in Los Angeles and Seoul, Roger Kingdom of the United States.

Evelyne Hall. Babe was nervous and made a false start. At the restart, perhaps because she was worried about disqualification for a second offense, Babe started slightly slower than Hall. Photographs of the race show Hall clearly ahead at the halfway mark. With her powerful strides, Babe pulled back the lead and they both finished in a new world record time of 11.7 seconds. But Babe was given the gold for a winning margin of 5 cm.

This result was followed by a silver in the high jump. Babe and fellow American Jean Shiley both jumped a new world record height. But, because the judges took exception at the last moment to Babe's style of jumping,

▲ Mildred "Babe" Didrikson (far right) winning the 80-m hurdles at the Games in Los Angeles, 1932. Babe is considered the greatest woman athlete of all time.

they awarded her the silver and Shiley the gold. Despite this setback, Babe won medals in running, jumping and throwing events—an unprecedented performance. Never mind that she had set new world records in doing so!

Later in life, Babe became a great golfer. When she was named the greatest woman athlete of the first half of this century by the American public, no one could have disagreed with this judgment.

The 400-m Hurdles

No man has ever dominated this chosen event so completely as American Edwin Moses. He won a gold medal in his first international 400-m hurdles race at the 1976 Montreal Olympics, at the age of only 20. Thereafter, he improved the world record and, though forced to miss the Moscow Games, carried on his single-minded pursuit. When the Los Angeles Games came around in 1984 he was able to pick up his well-deserved second gold medal.

Remarkably, four years later at Seoul, Moses was again the favorite, having been beaten at this distance only once in 11 years (122 straight races between 1977 and 1988). But,

unfortunately for Moses, the same dedication that had seen him through to his triumphs had also inspired his rivals. The American André Phillips, in a great performance, took Moses' title. Moses, however, did not give up his crown easily. He forced an Olympic record-breaking performance from Phillips, with himself ending in third place to El Hadj Dia Ba of Senegal. Of Moses, Phillips said: ''He's been my motivation, my incentive, my idol.''

▶ No accolade can truly do justice to the genius of Edwin Moses—the master of the 400-m hurdles.

▼ André Phillips (left) won the 400-m hurdles in Seoul.

RELAYS AND STEEPLECHASES

R elay races consist of teams of four athletes passing a baton to each other within a 10-m box after each runner has run his or her particular leg. Although these instructions sound quite straightforward, nothing at Olympic level is ever that simple.

Coordination is vital in relay races. The incoming runner must not find him- or herself either overrunning the next one or, worse, unable to catch him or her to pass the baton. Teams are often disqualified for passing the baton incorrectly. Not surprisingly, the United States, which has produced the largest number of sprinters, has won the 4 × 100 m event every time it has been staged — except for three occasions when the team was disqualified.

In 1988, Carl Lewis hoped to pick up a third gold medal in the 4 × 100 m relay. But he found that his team, in his absence, had been disqualified for passing the baton outside the box. Lee McNeill, who had replaced Carl Lewis in the heat, stepped out of the box when receiving from Calvin Smith. Afterwards McNeill blamed the bad exchange on his hand, saying that it was shaking with nerves so much it was a difficult target.

The relays have produced stunning individual legs. In Tokyo in 1964, for example, poor baton changing had left the American team 3 m behind, in fifth place, at the final change. Bob Hayes then produced a great burst of speed and won the race by an incredible 3 m.

▼ The trauma of the changeover in the men's 4 × 100 m relay.

Frank Wykoff of the United States, a member of the gold-winning team in Amsterdam in 1928 and Los Angeles in 1932, achieved a unique triple by winning again in Berlin in 1936. His name is not well known, however, because Olympic track history tends to remember teams rather than single performances.

The achievements of the Jamaicans over the years in short track events — especially the 400 m — cannot be ignored. At the London and Helsinki Games the Jamaicans took individual golds and silvers at 400 m. In the 1948 4 × 400 m relay, however, the 400-m gold medalist, Arthur Wint, pulled a muscle midrace and the team hopes were sunk. Four years later the same team literally prayed for victory before they took up position. The American team was strong, but the Jamaicans held on for the gold. They had a run that broke the 20-year-old record by

▲ Kip Keino soars through the air in the steeplechase.

4.3 seconds. So, after a four-year wait, the 4 × 400 m relay team finally did themselves justice in Helsinki in 1952.

The 3000-m Steeplechase

This race is an odd mixture of cross-country and hurdle racing. The athletes have to jump over 28 solid hurdles and 7 water jumps. It is an ungainly spectacle with runners stepping onto the hurdle to get over it. The awkwardness of the event was remarkably illustrated by Amos Biwott of Kenya in Mexico City in 1968. Without coaching or experience in the event, he used a jumping rather than hurdling style. This meant that he cleared the hurdles with his feet together. In the final, though ninth at the start of the last lap, he came through to win.

GLOSSARY

Antagonism Feelings of hostility or opposition.

Boycott To refuse to do something or to stay away from somewhere in order to make a point.

Consecutive Following on one after the other.

Controversial Likely to cause an argument.

Emphatic Expressed with firm and definite force.

Exceptional Someone or something that stands out from everyone or everything else.

Fascism The view held by Adolf Hitler that the Aryan race was superior to other races, especially Jews and blacks. In order to maintain his fascist system, Hitler aimed to control everything in Germany and to suppress all public criticism or opposition.

Homestretch The part of the race track between the last turn and the finish line.

Indelible Unable to be removed.

Inspiration Someone or something that gives great encouragement.

Invalidated Something that has been made no longer legal.

Olympiad The four-year period between each Olympic Games.

Participant Someone who takes part in something.

Prejudice Unfair opinions or feelings.

Propaganda Organized program for spreading opinions or ideas.

Prospective Expected or likely to happen.

Swastika A symbol—a cross with ends bent—used by followers of Adolf Hitler.

Tactics Plans to gain advantage.

Unprecedented Has never happened before.

FURTHER READING

Frommer, Harvey. *Olympic Controversies.* New York: Franklin Watts, 1987.

Glubock, Shirley, and Alfred Tamarin. *Olympic Games in Ancient Greece.* New York: Harper Junior Books, 1976.

Greenberg, Stan, ed. *The Guinness Book of Olympic Facts & Feats.* New York: Bantam, 1984.

Marshall, Nancy Thies. *Women Who Compete.* Old Tappan, N.J.: Fleming H. Revell Company, 1988.

Tatlow, Peter. *The Olympics.* New York: Franklin Watts, 1988.

Walczewski, Michael. *The Olympic Fun Fact Book.* New York: Dell, 1988.

Wallechinsky, David. *The Complete Book of the Olympics.* New York: Penguin Books, 1988.

INDEX